All Our
Wild Wonder

All Our Wild Wonder

Sarah Kay
Illustrated by Sophia Janowitz

hachette
BOOKS

NEW YORK   BOSTON

Hachette Books
Hachette Book Group
1290 Avenue of the Americas
New York, NY 10104
hachettebooks.com
twitter.com/hachettebooks

First edition: March 2018

Hachette Books is a division of Hachette Book Group, Inc.

The Hachette Books name and logo are trademarks of Hachette Book Group, Inc.

The publisher is not responsible for websites (or their content) that are not owned by the publisher.

LCCN: 2017956471
ISBNs: 978-0-316-38665-4 (hardcover), 978-0-316-38664-7 (ebook)

Printed in the United States of America

Phoenix Color

10 9 8 7 6 5 4 3 2 1

I was visiting a school in Northern India when I heard it for the first time in ages. It was barely audible above the shouting of children—the squeals and laughter bubbling from the schoolyard through the classroom windows. But it was there: the swish of silk saris and the jingle jangle of bangles on thin wrists like wind chimes.

This is what learning sounds like. I remember.

When I was five years old, the principal of my Junior School was Mrs. Ribeiro.

She was an Indian woman the size of a nightlight,
and she glided like a sailboat through the hallways of my school.

Once, when I got close enough to grab a fistful of her draping silk sari, I lifted it to try and see whether she had any feet at all.

I thought she floated.

We begged to be sent to her office—
the hanging plants like a jungle above our heads,
her quiet laughter.

Adults needed appointments, but we did not.
And even when she was in a "grown-up" meeting,
all it took was a gentle knock on the door, a peek
around the corner, and she was off, calling,

*Sorry dear. We'll have to reschedule. I have to see
someone else about a very important matter.*

It's about a gold star. It's about a new diorama.
It's about a finished reading book
(one level higher than last time!).

She visited every classroom,
knew every student by name.

She spoke to us like we were scholars.
Artists. Scientists. Athletes. Musicians.

And we were. My world was the size of a crayon box, and it took every color to draw her.

Once, on a New York City sidewalk, a group of women
in brightly colored saris walked by and someone shouted,
Look, Mom. Look at all those principals!

My world was the size of a classroom.
It was as tall as I could stretch my fingers, calling,
Please! Let me be the one to read to Mrs. Ribeiro.
Let me be the one to show her what I know.

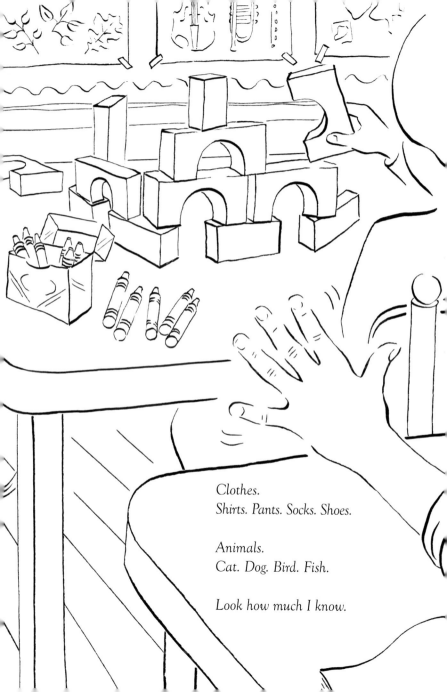

Clothes.
Shirts. Pants. Socks. Shoes.

Animals.
Cat. Dog. Bird. Fish.

Look how much I know.

She brought us guests and artists and a petting zoo.
They set up the cages in the parking lot

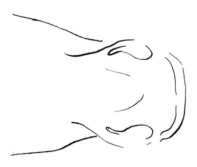

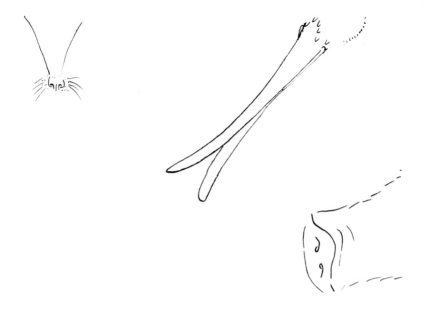

while we were still tucked up in our classrooms, unaware.
Rabbits and guinea pigs poked out their noses,

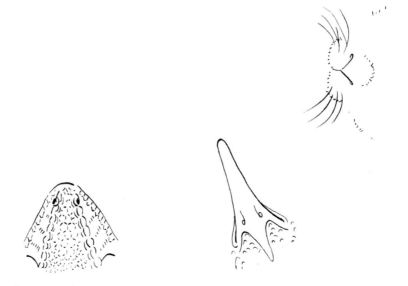

but Mrs. Ribeiro came to pause in front of the llama cage.

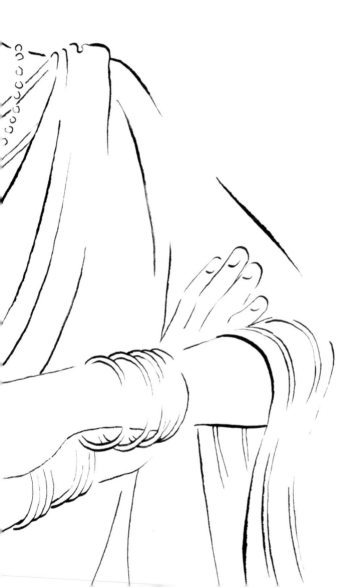

She and the llama considered each other for a long time.

She asked if he was tame enough to go inside.

The trainers laughed and told her, *Yeah he's plenty tame,*
but he doesn't know how to walk up stairs.

So she led him to the elevator.

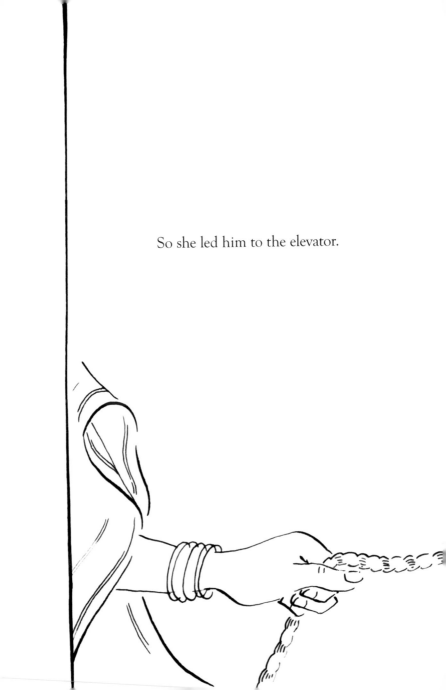

And when the doors slid open on the second floor,
there stood Mrs. Ribeiro in her bright pink sari,
with golden bangles and a llama on a leash.

She floated from classroom to classroom,
and we stared, cheered, laughed, and shouted.
We tugged at her sari, calling,
Miss, what is that? Where did it come from?

She made us wonder. She made us question.
She made us proud of what we had learned.

Clothes.
Shirts. Pants. Socks. Shoes. Saris.

Animals.
Cat. Dog. Bird. Fish. Llama.

Look how much I've learned.

She taught us to share.
She taught us to listen to each other
when someone else is speaking.
And then she let us go.

We were dandelion seeds released to the wind,
she asked for no return.
We are saplings now. With gentle hands.

The girl with bright cheeks and messy hair pins
now works at an orphanage in Cameroon.

The boy with the color-ordered markers
is now a graphic designer in Chicago.

The one with the best diorama
is now an animal activist in Argentina.

The one who loved to read out loud
is now a traveling poet.

She let us fly.

So I find myself at the front of a classroom.
My students tug at my sleeves and ask me,
Miss, are all poets so…weird?

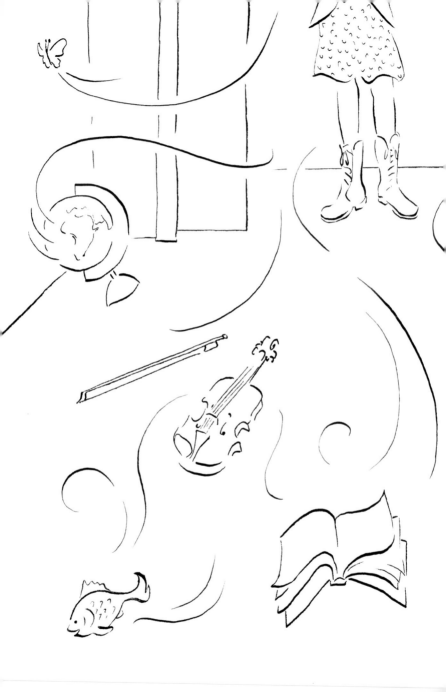

I pray for patience. I pray for wisdom—
to find a way to tame all the peculiar animals of this world,
to coax them enough to brave the elevator,
to see the doors slide open to my students' gaping mouths,
all their wild wonder.

They worry about everything.
They worry about what to write.
They worry about their grades.
They worry about who likes whom.
They talk over one another until I cannot hear them.
I tell them, *Listen.*

Listen to one another like you know you are scholars.
Artists. Scientists. Athletes. Musicians.

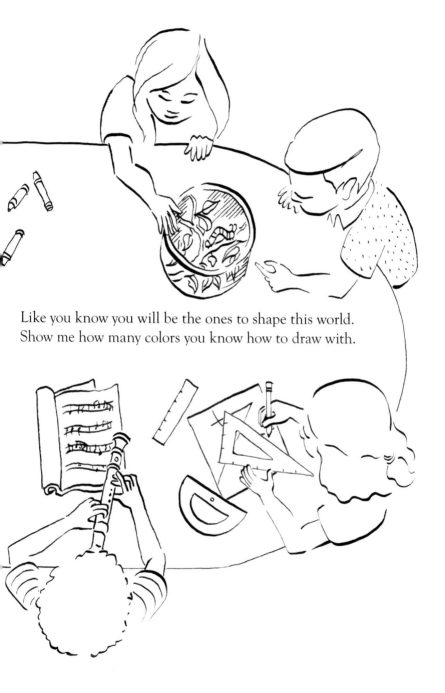

Like you know you will be the ones to shape this world.
Show me how many colors you know how to draw with.

Show me how proud you are of what you have learned.

And I promise I will do the same.

Acknowledgments

This book was made possible by: Sophia Janowitz, Sarah Wainwright, Joel Janowitz, Anne Lilly, Marianna Pease, Esther Burson, Molly Rubenstein, Laura Grigereit, Rachel Wasser, Mark Ostow, Blair Tate, Katrina Heron, Andrew Bellisari, Yfat Reiss-Gendell, Jan Kawamura-Kay, Jeffrey Kay, & PK.

With special thanks to Ms. Desmond, Mr. Kutner, Ms. Overall, Ms. Mathew, Mr. Banton, Ms. Downey, Mr. Siefring, Mr. Afshinnekkoo, Ms. Jacoby, Mrs. Ribeiro, and so many others, who have taught us within the classroom and beyond. Thank you for teaching us and for letting us fly.

About the Author
and Illustrator

Sarah Kay is the author of three additional poetry books: *No Matter the Wreckage*, *B*, and *The Type*. She is the founder and co-director of Project VOICE, an organization that brings spoken word poetry to schools and communities around the world. Sarah has been invited to share her poetry on such diverse stages as the 2011 TED Conference; the Malthouse Theatre in Melbourne, Australia; the Royal Danish Theatre in Copenhagen, Denmark; and Carnegie Hall in New York City, among hundreds of other venues around the world.

Sophia Janowitz has collaborated on four illustrated books of poetry with Sarah Kay. When she isn't drawing, Sophia designs typefaces, lights photo shoots, and edits essays. She recently received a master's degree in typography design at the École Estienne in Paris.